RHINO

vs.

HIPPO

BY
JERRY PALLOTTA
ILLUSTRATED BY
ROB BOLSTER

Scholastic Inc.

*The publisher would like to thank the following for their
kind permission to use their photographs in this book:*

Page 10 bottom image: Juniors / SuperStock; page 11 bottom image: AFP / Getty Images;
page 12 top image: www.skullsunlimited.com; page 13 top image: www.skullsunlimited.com;
page 14 center image: Martin Zwick / age fotostock / SuperStock; page 15 center image:
Victoria Stone & Mark Deeble / Getty Images; page 20 full-page image:
Chokniti Khongchum / Shutterstock; page 21 full-page image: vovol / Shutterstock.

To my pals Sean, Curran, and Marialice.
−J.P.
Thank you to M. C. Escher.
−R.B.

ISBN: 978-0-545-45191-8

45   24

Printed in the U.S.A.   40
First printing, January 2014

What would happen if a rhinoceros came face-to-face with a hippopotamus? What if they had a fight? Who do you think would win?

MEET A RHINO

Rhino is a shortened version of rhinoceros, which means "nose horn." They certainly do have horns. This is a white rhino.

FUN FACT
White rhinos cannot swim!

DID YOU KNOW?
The white rhino is the second-largest land mammal. Only elephants are bigger.

Scientific name: *Ceratotherium simum*

MEET A HIPPO

Hippo is a shortened version of hippopotamus. Hippopotamus means "river horse." From now on, we will call them rhino and hippo.

DEFINITION
A mammal is a warm-blooded animal with fur or hair that gives milk to its young.

Scientific name: *Hippopotamus amphibius*

TYPES OF RHINOS

There are five species of rhinos.

WHITE RHINO

LANGUAGE FACT
White rhino's name may have come from the Dutch word weid. *It means "wide," as in wide lips.*

COLOR FACT
White rhinos and black rhinos actually are both gray and look alike.

INDIAN RHINO

HORN FACT
Indian and Javan rhinos have only one horn.

BLACK RHINO

JAVAN RHINO

SUMATRAN RHINO

TYPES OF HIPPOS

There are two species of hippos.

HIPPOPOTAMUS

> **HEIGHT FACT**
> *The pygmy hippo is half as tall as a hippopotamus.*

PYGMY HIPPO

> **DID YOU KNOW?**
> *The pygmy hippo weighs only one-fourth as much as a hippo.*

WHITE RHINO TERRITORY

White rhinos live in Africa.

AFRICA

where white rhinos lived originally

where white rhinos have been reintroduced ✖

DID YOU KNOW?
Rhinos have been on earth for 50 million years.

FUN FACT
Rhinos live in grasslands and savannas.

DEFINITION
A savanna is a grassy area with few trees.

HIPPO TERRITORY

Hippos also live in Africa.

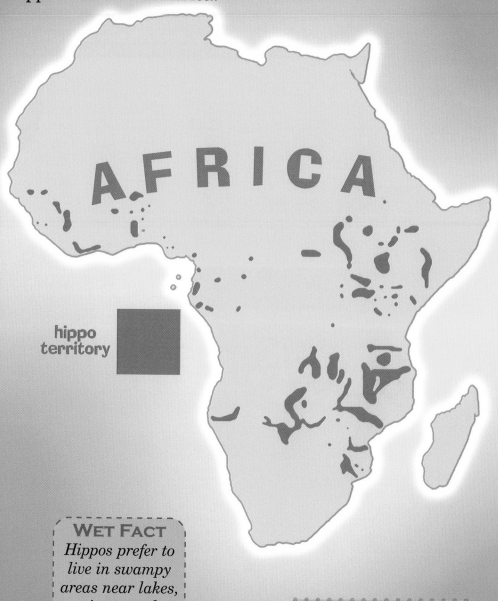

AFRICA

hippo territory

WET FACT
Hippos prefer to live in swampy areas near lakes, rivers, and streams.

DID YOU KNOW?
Resting in water helps hippos stay cool.

RHINO DIET

White rhinos eat grass. Grass, grass, and more grass. Rhinos are not meat eaters; they have no interest in eating a hippo. White rhinos have wide lips. They pull up grass with their lips. They chew the grass with their back molars.

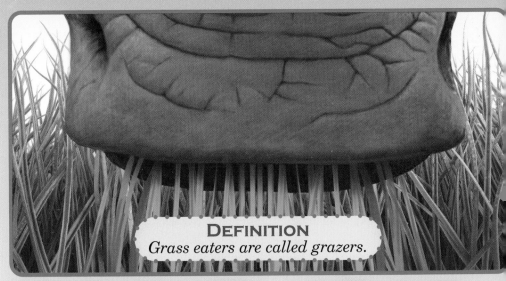

DEFINITION
Grass eaters are called grazers.

RHINO BABY

This is a baby rhino.

TUMMY FACT
A rhino has four sections to its stomach. It takes a lot to digest grass.

FUN FACT
When rhinos are born, they can weigh up to 90 pounds.

HIPPO DIET

Hippos also eat grass and some leaves. They prefer to eat at night. They rest during the day.

FACT
Areas that have been eaten by hippos are called "hippo lawns."

HIPPO BABY

Which is cuter? A baby hippo or rhino?

DID YOU KNOW?
A baby hippo weighs between 60–100 pounds.

RHINOCEROS SKELETON

A rhinoceros is a vertebrate animal. Vertebrates have backbones just like humans.

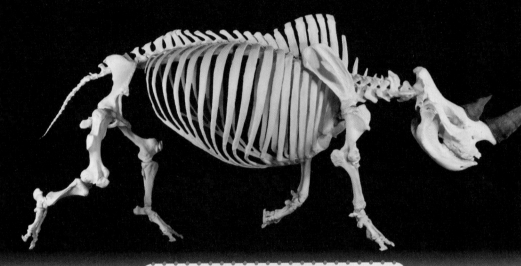

This insect shares its name with the rhino.

HIPPOPOTAMUS SKELETON

A hippo is also a vertebrate. Its spinal cord runs from its brain to its tail.

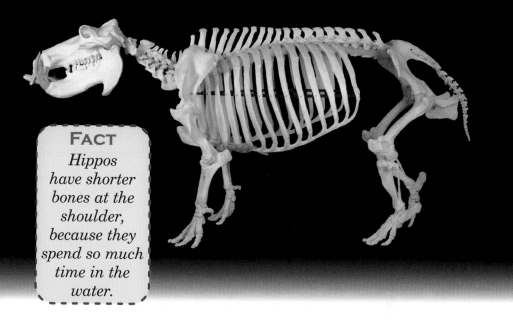

FACT
Hippos have shorter bones at the shoulder, because they spend so much time in the water.

This is a hippopotamus beetle.

FACT?
The hippo beetle's scientific name is Royis wandelirius.

DID YOU KNOW?
One of the insects on these two pages is fake. Which one?

FREE RIDE

How would you like to ride around on a rhino? That is what oxpeckers do. These birds eat ticks, fleas, blood-sucking flies, and insect larvae off the backs of rhinos.

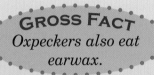

GROSS FACT
Oxpeckers also eat earwax.

FUN FACT
Oxpeckers are also called tickbirds.

COLOR FACT
Oxpeckers are easy to recognize; they have red eyes and red beaks.

Oxpeckers live only where there are larger mammals. They also like to ride on cattle, giraffes, zebra, and buffalo. Some scientists think it is a mutual relationship in which rhino and oxpecker both benefit. Others think the bird is a parasite.

FREE CLEANING

The hippo loves the water. One reason might be the carp that clean its teeth, hide, and lips.

Hippos love freshwater, and so do humans. This sometimes creates conflicts between people and hippos.

RHINO FOOT

A rhino foot has three toes.

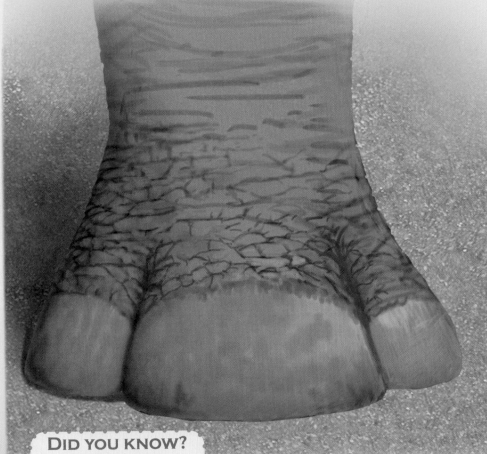

DID YOU KNOW?
An elephant foot has five toes.

Largest land mammal

Second-largest land mammal

elephant

rhino

HIPPO TOES

A hippo foot has four toes.

Third-largest land mammal

hippo

Largest mammal: blue whale

human

RHINO WEAPONS

A rhino's best weapon is its size. It is huge! Rhinos stand six feet high at the shoulders and weigh 8,000 pounds.

FUN FACT
The rhino's horn is made of keratin. Keratin is the same material your hair and fingernails are made of.

4 TONS

DID YOU KNOW?
8,000 pounds equals 4 tons.

HIPPO WEAPONS

The hippo's best weapons are its huge teeth and strong jaw. It has six big front teeth on its upper jaw and four teeth plus two long tusks on its lower jaw. It chews with its back molars.

FACT

Elephants, hippos, walrus, and wild boars have tusks.

DEFINITION

A tusk is a long, pointed tooth. Tusks are usually found in pairs.

3 TONS

A hippo's size is also a great weapon!

RHINO SKIN

Rhinos are mammals but they have almost no hair.

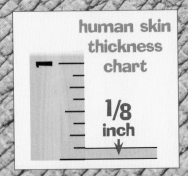

human skin thickness chart

1/8 inch

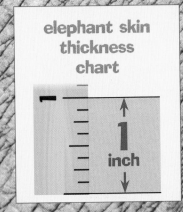

elephant skin thickness chart

1 inch

HIPPO SKIN

Hippos also have almost no hair.

IT'S NOT BLOOD!
Hippos have a natural skin lotion. Their skin oozes a reddish-orange oil.

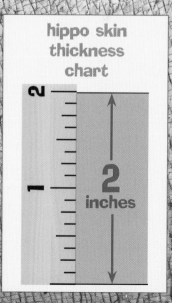

white rhino skin thickness chart

1
1½ inches

hippo skin thickness chart

2
1
2 inches

I HEAR YOU

The rhino can swivel its ears in different directions. It has excellent hearing.

DEFINITION
A group of rhinos is called a crash.

DID YOU KNOW?
A rhino can smell and hear a lion before it sees it.

I SEE YOU

The hippo's head is beautifully designed. When swimming, its ears, nose, and eyes are above water. It is always on the lookout.

DEFINITION

A group of hippos is called a bloat.

DID YOU KNOW?

A hippo can sleep underwater. While sleeping, it surfaces every five minutes to breathe.

RHINO SPEED

In short bursts, a rhino can run 30 miles per hour.

SPEED LIMIT 30

RUNNING FACT
A rhino can easily outrun a human.

FUN FACT
A rhinoceros can gallop like a horse.

HIPPO SPEED

A hippo can run about 18 miles per hour. A hippo has no interest in running a marathon. It's not designed for long-distance running.

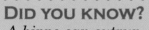

DID YOU KNOW?
A hippo can outrun most humans.

DID YOU KNOW?
According to zoologists, the closest known relatives to hippos are dolphins and whales.

DEFINITION
A zoologist is a scientist who studies animals and animal behavior.

LISTEN!

I told the illustrator not to show the rhino's rear end, but he did!

Dear Rob,
I don't think
it's a good idea
to show the
rhino's rear end!
Jerry

DID YOU KNOW?
The tail of a rhino has no significant function.

DON'T DO IT!

I asked the illustrator not to show the hippo's rear end, either!

Rob,

I think the editor and the art director are upset that you showed the hippo's rear end!

Jerry

JERRY,
I'M THE ART DIRECTOR.
PLEASE LEAVE ME ALONE!
ROB

DID YOU KNOW?
From behind, the hippo and the rhino look similar.

The hippo has a small tail. It's not long like a snow leopard tail, not fluffy like a horse tail, and not good for balance like a kangaroo tail.

The thirsty rhino walks over to the watering hole.

As the rhino takes a drink, the hippo opens its mouth and scares the rhino away. The thirsty rhino tries again. The hippo opens its big mouth, and the frightened rhino backs off.

Later, the hippo wants a drink. This time, the rhino charges and chases the hippo. The hippo returns. The rhino lowers its head and flashes its horns, and the hippo runs away.

Rhinos don't eat hippos. Hippos don't eat rhinos. But they are fighting for the same water.

Again the hippo opens its mouth, and the rhino runs away.

The rhino returns and charges the hippo. At the last second, the hippo turns around and opens its powerful jaws. The rhino retreats.

The rhino slowly walks back, with its head down and horns ready. The hippo swings around quickly and bites the rhino on its hind leg. Ouch! The rhino's leg is broken. It limps away.

The rhino has made a fatal mistake.

WHO HAS THE ADVANTAGE?
CHECKLIST

RHINO		HIPPO
☐	Weight	☐
☐	Size	☐
☐	Weapons	☐
☐	Skin	☐
☐	Ears	☐
☐	Swimming ability	☐
☐	Speed	☐

Author note: This is one way the fight might have ended.
How would you write the ending?